Little White Bird

Bonnie L. Dunlap

ISBN 979-8-88616-903-4 (paperback)
ISBN 979-8-88616-904-1 (digital)

Christian Faith Publishing
832 Park Avenue
Meadville, PA 16335
www.christianfaithpublishing.com

Printed in the United States of America

What The?

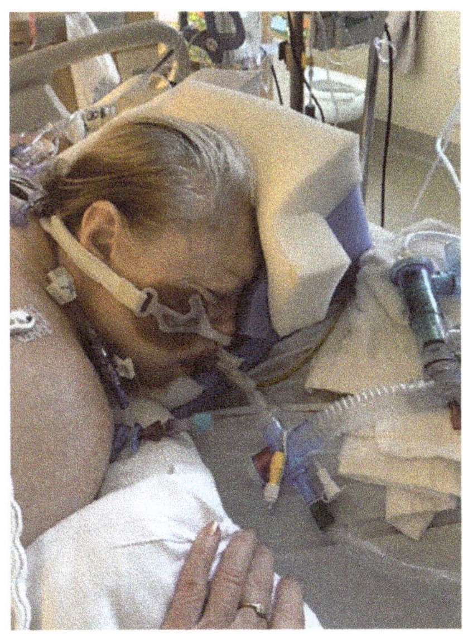

I remember opening my eyes and seeing my daughter, Tiffany, leaning over me! My husband, Dave, was standing at the foot of my hospital bed. "Mom! Do you know where you are?" I said *no* or rather shook my head *no*. "You are at the Asante Hospital in Medford, Oregon. You are going to be okay, Mom. You are strong, but you are very sick. You got the worst kind of pneumonia, pneumococcal pneumonia. The good news is that it is treatable with time. You also have sepsis; you are going to have a trek and no voice box, and you won't be able to talk."

I remember thinking, *What the hell.* I don't believe this is happening to me. I don't remember how I got here.

All I could do is move my right hand and arm and wiggle my toes! My left hand looked like a dead "trout" and the same color so big and flat, and it felt like it weighed 150 pounds. I called it "the blob" like a bad scary movie. I asked, "Why can't I move my left hand and arm?" My daughter knew the answer right off of what happened, being a doctor in physical therapy nerve damage.

"It's called brachial plexus," she said. "It happened while you were placed in a prone position for too long while you were on a ventilator." I was told that I was on or off of it for three weeks. I remember being so angry! I told everyone to fuck off and that I hate you people. I felt like I was cast in cement—feeling trapped and helpless.

My daughter and my husband understood my anger and so did the nurses. I was told I had gone into A-fib, my heart stopped, code blue alerted, and I died. My angels were working overtime. A miracle in the making, that I shouldn't have survived. They said I was a tough old bird and not ready to die! Dave said, "Honey, you will have quite the story to tell," and when I thought I was ready, they would share the beginning of the story. I am still in shock and cannot believe what is happening to me. My Dave and Tiffany would be there every time I opened my eyes, and eventually, little things would come back to me.

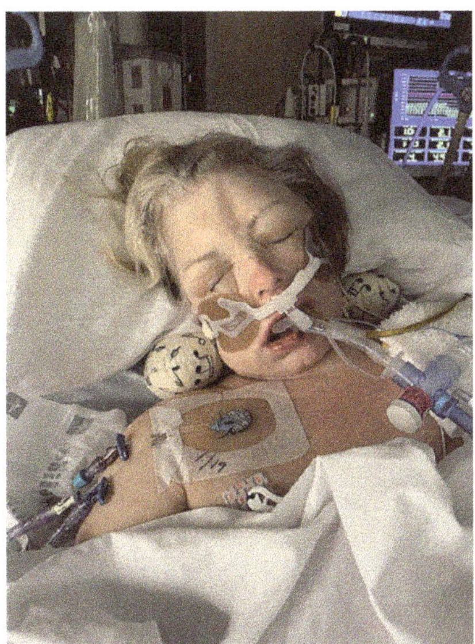

I remember the doctor telling me that he needs to put a tube down my throat and that I needed a ventilator to help me breathe.

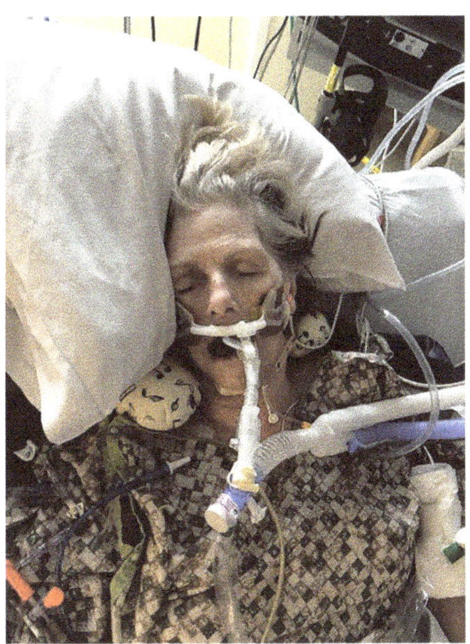

I remember shaking my head *no*, but then I heard Tiffany say, "Mom, we need to do this to keep you alive!"

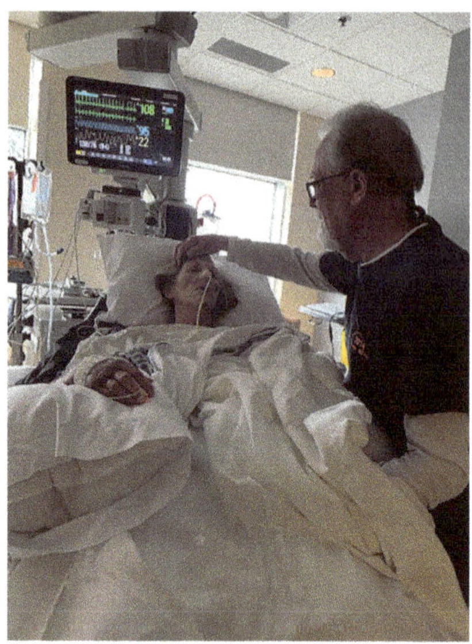

I said, "Okay." Then I remember feeling Dave's hand when he rubbed it across my forehead. I remember hearing, "I love you so much. Come on now and get well." I remember my sister's voice and her telling the nurse how I was a hairdresser and still doing hair at age seventy-three which I was not yet; I was still seventy-two. Then I heard her telling another nurse how I was a Miss Teenage America semi-finalist and I sang "Getting to Know You." I was her beautiful sister! She would tell me every day about how well I was doing and she was so proud of me. I, again, little by little, remember things and dreams. I still would gather my thoughts and try to remember what happened to me. Why me? I am still in disbelief.

My morning would start with nurses coming in the ICU room, chest X-rays, medicines, blood pressure, take my temperature, and put this injection of what looked like a strawberry milkshake into a feeding tube that went into my stomach and then vial of water potassium and nutrients.

For one month, thirty days, no water or food. I remember telling Dave, "I am so thirsty. May I please have some water?" He would say that I couldn't have any. I was so hungry. Dave and Tiff would come into the ICU to see me, and they would each have their waters and coffee. I wanted it so bad. My lips felt like five layers of cardboard! My nurses would say *no* to me. I think that's when I told them, "I hate you people!" Then would come the shot that burned and stung into my stomach. Then would come the drawing of blood, followed by "here comes the poke in the finger" morning and night. Every finger on my right hand was black and blue. Let's not forget that everything was done with the right hand and arm.

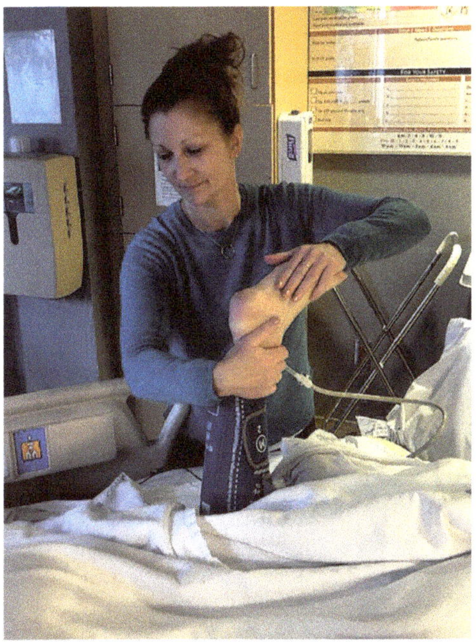

My daughter would drive seven hours back to Santa Cruz to be with my grandchildren, Lucas and Alivia. She would have them in her care Monday, Tuesday, and Wednesday, then drive back to the hospital to be with me while her ex, their father, would care for them Thursday, Friday, and Saturday, then she would leave to go back Sunday. She would do this for seven weeks. Just a few miles put on her Cadillac. Dave would be there 6:00 a.m. to 6:00 p.m. at night encouraging me on, telling me that I was a fighter and he was so proud of me.

One of the most feelings of helplessness was having to go to the bathroom peeing in a catheter but pooping would be in a bedpan.

Always rolling to the left side of the bed but on the wounded arm; it was very painful and humiliating. They, the nurses, would cheer me on and tell me how good I was doing four hundred butt wipes later. Oh my god, I swear some of my male nurses were just young boys. I swear, they were only fourteen years old. LOL, just kidding. They would undress you, sponge bath you, put you on the bedpan, wipe your butt, tuck you in, and make you as comfortable as possible. They would come in and rearrange you and your blankets every two hours and throughout the night, as again I was still feeling that I was cast in cement or at least I felt that way and could not move by myself. Two nurses would come in and say, "One, two, three," and they would pull the pad underneath me and pull me back up in the bed as I would keep sliding down in the bed.

The hardest thing to witness for Dave, Tiffany, and my sister was to witness how helpless and frustrating it was for me. In would come the horrible breathing treatments. They would put this tube in my mouth, and it would spin and make a terrible noise and had a god-awful taste! My doctor would bring in nebulizers breath and lung treatments. My respiratory specialists would apologize to me as they knew how hard they were to get through, but the lungs had to be treated this way. My favorite doctor was Dr. Maguel, and he would always enter the room saying, "I know, I know, I am sorry!"

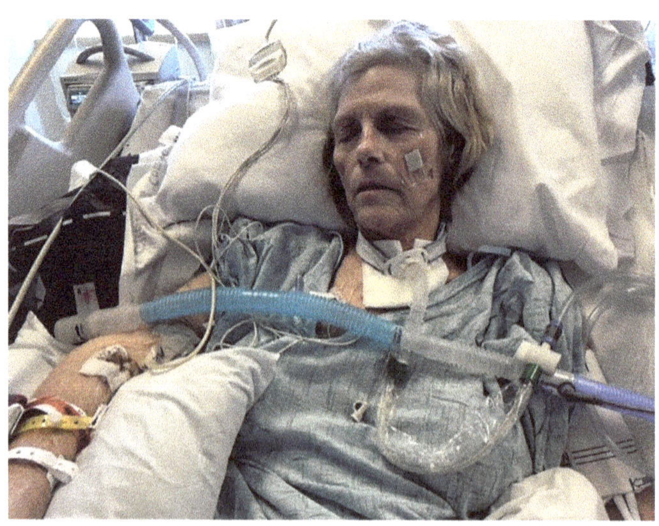

Bonnie Dunlap continues to make me proud!! She hates that tube down her throat and hates being stuck in bed. We were Lucky the day nurse found the right cocktail of sedation to allow you to settle down and 'breath'.
Tracheostomy is planned for tomorrow and then we will focus on building her strength. She is so unbelievably weak!!
Thank you to those who pray and continue to pray. And thank you Laura Hamby for coming today, for your support and for the prayer circle!!!!
Much love!!!

The next step would be to put in the tracheostomy tube which meant going without a voice box, and I would have to use a word board to communicate. It was very frustrating to point to letters trying to make words, and it was quite the guessing game for family. The worst part of having a trek was the gagging from the phlegm and hardship in trying to breath. They would have to suck out the phlegm and pump your throat to keep it clear so I wouldn't drown. It was god-awful. I remember praying, "Please, God, let me be done with this!" It was so scary and so hard to endure. I would breathe like Darth Vader *pushhhooooo*. I sounded like him too, blow breath out and breath in full of hot air.

All of a sudden, I would start to snore; the noise would come out of my throat. So weird. Doctors would cover the trek hole with Band-Aid type dressing that I would have to press my good hand against to make noise or words come out. They would change the Band-Aids every morning and pull my skin; taking them off hurt so bad.

Finally, they came up with an idea—thanks to nurse Nancy, the wound nurse—to put a lace necklace over the gauze so as not to rip my skin. In the beginning, doctors found a pediatric trek button to plug the hole as my neck was so tiny. The good news is the trek did not have to stay in for very long, and by the time I left rehab, the hole where the Trek had been was totally healed and the scab had fallen, and for the first time in a long time, I was happy that I had wrinkles in my neck as you cannot see where the trek was! I will never forget that experience, and I am so grateful that I had a nurse come into talk with me and share her story of when she had been in a car accident and was in the hospital for nine months. She, too, had to have a tracheostomy to save her life. Her lungs were also threatened; she had several broken bones, and ribs had punctured her lungs! Looking at her, she was so pretty and would never have guessed she had an awful experience like that. This gave me such hope, and all of a sudden, I realized that this too would pass, and I would get better; this would just be a bad memory. She was so inspiring to me, and so when I can, I plan to visit patients going through this ordeal to let them know it will all be okay and hopefully be an inspiration to help them have hope and that it will not be forever and it will just seem like a bad dream! I am so grateful I had her for a nurse that night as she wasn't scheduled to work that night, but someone had called in sick, and she took her place and gave me grace!

Eventually, Dave and Tiffany would take shifts. Dave would time in 6:00 a.m. to 6:00 p.m. Tiff would come in 7:00 a.m. until the evening shift change; she would help with working with PTs helping me to transfer on slide board to transfer from wheelchair to bed. Libby, my sister, would come every day around 3:30. I remember waiting to hear her voice from the very first day until she got the flu while I was in rehab the last two weeks and couldn't come to visit me or Kevin, her husband! Oh, that's right, family discount? After I had been transferred to Intermediate Care Unit (IMCU), Libby was visiting me when she got the call from the police that her husband, Kevin Jack, had been in a motorcycle accident and was in Asante Hospital. I heard her say I'm just leaving there, so back in she went down the stairs to emergency ward. Kevin was hit straight on by a Silverado pick-up truck! He was on his motorcycle in the left lane waiting to make a turn. There was a car in front of him, so he could not move forward. The driver of the truck made his turn into the gas station, and cutting it too close, he hit Kevin, and his bike leaned to the right, but the front wheel grabbed his left leg and dragged it and him under the truck. A passerby saved his life with tourniquet as blood spurted out of the main artery.

The driver of the truck was twenty-five years old and driving with suspended license! Kevin ended up with five surgeries to save his leg; a miracle he was alive, and he was happy they could save his leg. He broke his bones in femur and tabula; he had four rods and pealing of the skin and very painful wound care of scrapping off dead skin scales; Libby would now be with him every day and me in the evenings. He ended up in rehab, just down the hall from me. What were the odds of that happening? He would come to my room in his wheelchair, and we would talk and cry and commiserate with each other. A crazy way to get closer to someone, but I have to say that it helped us both to share our story and journey together, and we didn't have to go through rehab alone. We would be together in the gym, working hard to walk, stand, and build muscle and strength while encouraging each other. We would meet in the dining room for dinner unless he had wound care or surgery, in which case I ate in my room. We also had an evening when the whole family had dinner together in the dining room. Tiff and Libby picked up sushi and Mexican food from our favorite restaurants, a real treat to bring food from the outside. Kevin ended up getting the flu also and was two weeks in rehab without his wife (my sister Libby), which was so hard on both of them. He finally got to go home to start his rehabilitation with home care. He and I said if anyone had told us at our open house parties which were such a wonderful celebrations in our new homes with friends and neighbors before the New Year 2020. We would have never believed what was going to happen to us and our family in a split second; everything changed for all of us. A rude awakening not to take your life for granted as it can change in a blink of an eye.

Reflections back too IMCU; family, Dave, and Tiff would chat every day on Facebook and text every fifty-seven days the experience of this incredible journey. When I was strong enough, they started to share pictures from the beginning of what happened to me! It is crazy weird; what was real and what wasn't? I keep having questions. Was I hallucinating or dreaming? Or did this really happen? I remember having to go poop, and we were all sitting in a hallway that I guess was in a hospital, and I asked someone—I guess it was my daughter—to take me to the bathroom; there were all kinds of people around, and my pulmonary doctor wanted to give me that god-awful breathing treatment that spun in my mouth. Dave was sitting next to me, and people were coming in and out of side doorway. Tiffany said, "Just go, Mom, if you have to go, *just go*! According to Dave when I asked him about this, I had a tube up my butt that went under the bed and in a container. I dreamed it was a trough that went under the bed and out somewhere. I remember just pooping in front of all these people. Crazy, crazy, crazy. I was either on a bedpan at night or on catheter. When I was off catheter, I had a foley. They started measuring how much pee was in my bladder by taking ultrasound.

When I got to rehab, they wanted me to start peeing by myself and started me on the drug Flomax to start things going. I had been on a catheter for so long that my body forgot how to eliminate urine on my own. Once I started peeing, they would have to take an ultrasound of my stomach to see if I had more than 400c as urinary infections could occur, so in which case, they would have to do a straight catheter again and put in at night. I was so happy when I started peeing everything out on my own and going to the big girl potty and not the bedpan or bedside commode, but my own hygiene of simple wiping. Good God, so many cold butt wipes later, and so humiliating, but necessary. I would have to call the nurse in at 3:00 a.m. for the bedside commode, then they would have to help me out of bed and lift me with a gate belt wrapped around the waist yet above the food peg in my stomach and lift me up and onto the bedside commode and then they would leave me sitting there until I was done and hit the nurses call button when done. They would rearrange my bedding, fluff up my pillow, put back on my bed boots to keep feet straight and ankles strong, and then tuck me back in bed and measure pee again!

I remember being out in the hallway and thinking to myself, *Gee, these are the greatest beds,* you could just crap, and it goes out under the bed and into that special trough, and no matter where I was in the hospital, I could just let her rip. So weird, weird, weird,

weird. I also dreamed that my niece, Holly, who is a school teacher, was one of the specialist called in with this same group of people that day, and she was there to help me talk and with my speech. I asked Dave about this dream; he told me that no, there was no Holly, but there was a nurse named Holly that took care of me. I guess it was the drugs!

The Cad Chair

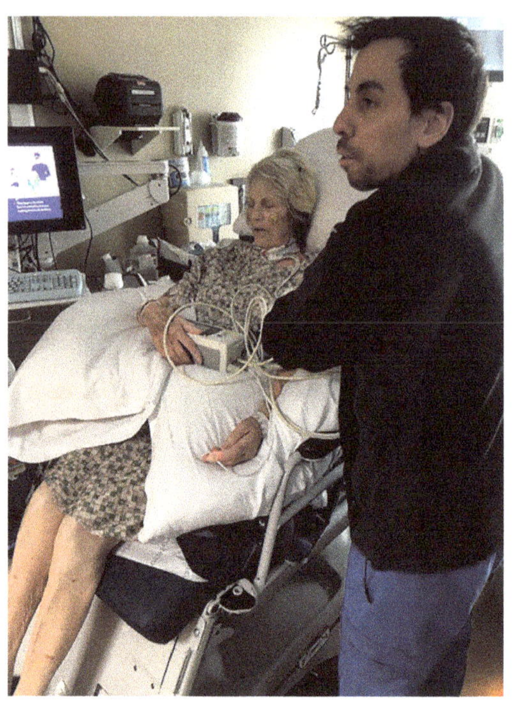

B ack in the ICU room, I had a nurse named John. He was so sweet; once I was sitting up, he put me in a big chair on wheels called the cad chair, and he would take me out of the ICU room and give me a ride up and down the halls of the hospital. It was so fun. I remember how free it felt to be in that chair. He felt it was very important that I do that whenever I could. I remember looking out of the room and into the hall and there would be someone watching me at all times through a small window outside my room. They, too, would have their drinks of water or coffee. I just remember wanting something to drink all the time. Finally, someone dipped a sponge stick in water and gave it to me to suck on.

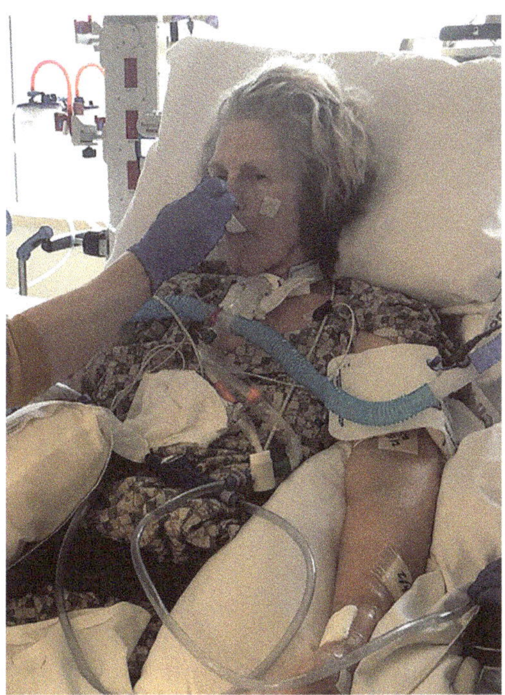

I think it was February 28; they gave me ice chips. My speech therapist came in with water and ice chips. Oh, it was so good; those ice chips tasted so wonderful. Then I got to sip water from a straw, and then oh my gosh, she had a spoon and applesauce. I remember that applesauce tasted so amazing. The first food taste since January 17; so good! I can eat food again, and from that day on, I started out with a bowl of tomato soup, very tricky to eat, and it went everywhere as my hand was so wobbly and shaky to even hold a spoon, but I didn't care. I then graduated to baby food then to solid food: puddings, Jell-O, ice cream, applesauce, protein shakes, and finally, I got my tea. I asked every nurse I had for some tea, and they would always tell me no. Now finally, I got orange spice tea with honey. Heavenly days. I also got started with breakfasts, lunch, and dinner. Oh my god, the food at Asante Hospital was fantastic. Once I got to rehab, I could order from special menu or off the main menu, but I usually went for the main menu because they would bring you a little bit of everything to try; for instance, with breakfast, you would have coffee, orange juice, milk, oatmeal, scrambled eggs, bacon, orange slice, toast, and blueberry muffin! So much to choose from off your tray. Same at lunch: meatloaf and mashed potatoes, gravy, fruit bowl, salad, and always a dessert. Same at dinner: salads, dinner roll, BBQ steak, different potatoes, and different delicious desserts. I was quite spoiled with fabulous cooks. A real treat to look forward to. Right on schedule, everyday breakfast is 7:30. Lunch is at 12:00 and dinner is at 5:00. The nurses would have to cut my meat, open my milk carton, straws, lids, salt, and pepper packets as I only had use of one hand and arm. A real pain in my side, but they made sure to take care of me if Dave or my daughter wasn't there to do it at night as they had to go home sometimes to sleep! LOL.

In the Beginning

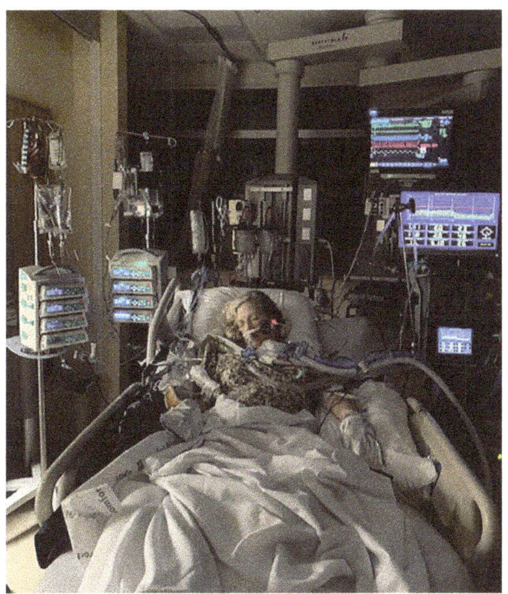

 **Tiffany Leamer-Thornton**
27 mins ·

Update on mom: They figured out the strain of bacteria and have started the antibiotics it is sensitive to. She spent the entire day face down and at 5:30pm the intensivist wanted to try for a CT scan of her lungs to better view what we are dealing with. So they put her face up and after 2 hours of getting poor oxygen readings, they decided she is too fragile to be moved to radiology. She will continue to be heavily monitored with her 1 on 1 nurse tonight. Plans are to prone her again at midnight.
*she a fighter....that's my mom!

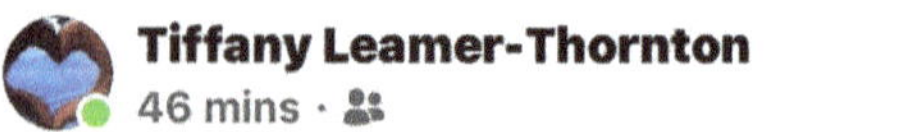

Tiffany Leamer-Thornton
46 mins ·

Day 15 with Bonnie Dunlap. Theme of the day; welcome to the roller coaster AND slow deep breaths mom!
After a night of rest she is now struggling to breath. A radial arterial line was put back in to monitor her blood pressure as her skin can't tolerate the pressure from a blood pressure cuff. She's finally getting an anti-arithmetic med to get her out of a-fib, flutter, brady-, and tachycardia. Her left arm has a brachial plexus injury (google it) from when she was positioned on her stomach a couple days ago. She will most likely have a tracheostomy put in later today.
Hardest part is watching her struggle, seeing the fear in her eyes and not being able to help her.
Today is not a good day:(

On January 17th, 2020, Dave makes the 911 call. I had been home from urgent care; I was sent home two days prior with Ibuprofen; they gave me a flu test, and they said that I did not have the flu, so they sent me home and said that it was a virus; they didn't take a blood test or even take my temperature. I probably had sepsis at the time; if they had tested my blood, they would have seen it! You know that flu test with the long Q tip seven inches shoved up your nostril burns like hell and feels like they hit your brain? Anywho, I didn't remember the 911 call or paramedics putting me in ambulance or the ride to three rivers hospital in Grants pass or the two days there or when my daughter flew in to be with me. I didn't know of the ride with her in the ambulance and the mercy flight when they transferred me to the Asante Hospital in Medford as they had the ventilator I needed. Dave followed behind in his car, and as he told me later, he stopped off at the house to feed our Bella kitty before meeting up with us; I remember none of this! Only after I was stronger did my Dave, Tiffany, Libby, and Kevin would show me pictures of me hooked to so many tubes ventilator and three trees with four different kinds of antibiotics hanging on each one of them and all were going into me. Little bits and pieces while looking at pictures, I would remember hearing their voices; to this day now, I am at home doing really well; I still have bits and pieces coming back remembering the dreams exactly when that happened. My near-death experience!

Knocking on Heaven's Door

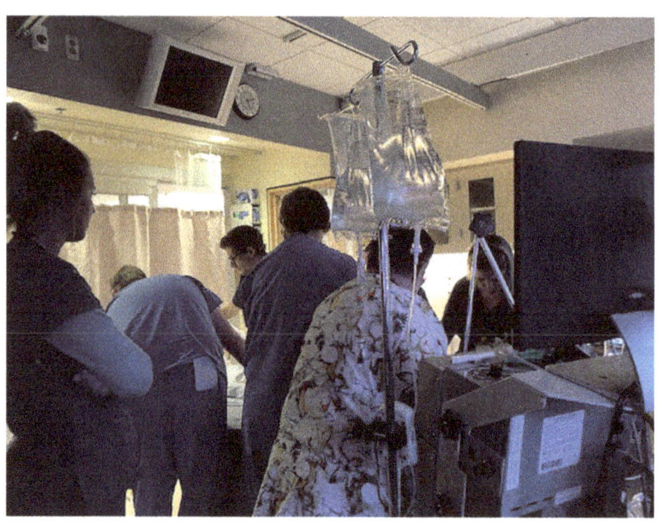

Tiffany Leamer-Thornton
14 mins · 👥

Sunday update on **Bonnie Dunlap**: it's been a very eventful morning.... she may have a GI bleed somewhere. They will keep checking her blood every 4 hours. If her hematocrit keeps dropping they will do a blood transfusion and possibly an endoscopy to take a look. She just had her entire team in the room on 2 different events as her oxygen saturation's blood pressure, and heart rate tanked. Not sure what or why. Maybe a mucous plug but RT can't find it.

Hour-by-hour is the theme of the day.

Thank you all for your thoughts and prayers. We need all of them!

I was in my nanny and pappy's house. My pappy built this house. He was a carpenter, and my mom, her sister (my Aunt Bonnie), whom I was named after, and her younger brother (my uncle Bud), were born in the front bedroom with a midwife to help my nana. I was born in Red Bluff, California, at St. Elizabeth's Hospital on May 21, 1947. I was brought home to this house. Nanny and Pappy's house was one of my favorite places to be, and where I loved to spend all my hot summers growing up along with my brother and sister. In my dream, I would remember them all. The things we did we helped Nanny cook, hung clothes on the line, the clothes pins, and the smell of fresh clean sheets when taking them off the clothesline. Ironing the pillowcases and setting the table. Walking to town seeing cousins that lived right around the corner and up the hill. The best times ever!

I would picture me at the dining room table, and on Sundays, aunties would be invited for fried chicken or pot roast with full on China and white tablecloths. I remember my pappy pouring his tea out of his teacup and into his saucer and then slurping it into his mouth. I used to love to watch him. In the winter months, a fire always in the dining room fireplace where we would dress and undress as children to stay warm. With all these flashbacks, I am now in my favorite living room; and all of a sudden, sparkles of stars appeared and filled the room. They turned into all my loved ones that had died and gone to heaven. There they stood circled around me was my father, my Aunt Evelyn(his sister), my Aunt Bonnie, Uncle Bob, Uncle buddy, my closest and dearest cousin, Cathy, and my nanny and pappy. They were all standing around me. I was looking everywhere for my mom, and then I heard her say, "I am here in you and with you and surround you always." I guess that's why I hear her come out of my mouth sometimes! LOL. They say that when your time is near, you have a welcoming party greet you and escort you to heaven! That's when I got it! Souls don't take up a lot of room. God gives us all unique DNA, none of us have the same identity, and it is said that you will see and recognize your loved ones in heaven. I remember feeling so much love. God is love! God was there!

Little White Bird

I was never afraid, and I knew why everyone was there. God knew how much I loved life, my husband Dave, my family, grandchildren, and great grandchild. I had my faith in God and I knew he was there. God was there! All of a sudden, there was a ray of bright white light, and I saw a bird, it was a little white bird, a dove (it looked like the one on my favorite sweater). This little dove looked so white, bright, and beautiful with diamonds for eyes. This dove flew into this picture of all of us in my nanny's living room and just like a freeze frame, like a computer picture. I was to choose and click on the picture that I wanted. The picture on the left was me and my family, and on the right was the little white bird looking now like the blue tweet bird on our modern-day phone but only white and sitting the opposite way. I wasn't ready to go with my loved ones that had gone on before me. I knew I was dreaming this at the very time I was dying, and I didn't even know or remember being on the ventilator the first three weeks in the hospital when trying to keep me alive.

They say life flashes before your very eyes before you die, but mine went really slow. I remember being three years old and being in the backyard playing in the mud behind a white house in Long Beach where we lived; it was just me with Mommy and Daddy when he was stationed in the service after World War 2. I remember being the only child as there was no sister Libby yet. I was alone in the yard, and I would go and peek in the windows of this white building off the patio. I would see a round table with chairs all around and poker chips and cards sitting on top of the table (as my mom told me later). Daddy would play poker with his friends once a month on poker night! I remember taking a nap beside my mom; I was lying next to her on the bed and watched her try to sleep in between me talking. She would give me stuff to do to keep me quiet like her jewelry box. I remember seeing all her treasures, and it made me happy. Then

I would flashback to listening to lullabies as my nanny and mom, in that favorite living room, rock me in that fabulous rocker nanny had and my favorite songs that they sang to me. I could hear them singing to me as they held me. "Rock-a-bye Baby" and "It's an Irish Lullaby." I especially liked the part hearing "To ra lu ra lu ra. To ra lu ra li to ra lu ra lu ra, hush now, don't you cry. When Irish eyes are smiling that's an Irish lullaby!"

From there, my mind went to a place of my childhood, our home on 32nd Avenue. I remember growing up there when I was five years old until the fifth grade, and my best friend Christine Ladley (I called her Krissy) lived right next door. We had moved from Long Beach to nanny and pappy's house where my sister suddenly appeared and became a part of my young life, and I was not alone any longer. We then moved to Sacramento to the first house my parents bought—the one on 32nd Avenue. I would walk through the rooms of the house remembering the bird wallpaper with a pink background on the wall in the living room. The 50s pink leather sectional sofa had three sections. Mom would reposition them and change the furniture around, and I loved it when she would do that and then every morning upon seeing it, I would be surprised all over again. I started seeing myself sitting on that sofa with my nanny, with my little dolls, coffee cup filled with milk and sugar mostly, and a splash of coffee my nanny made just for me. I would wait with anticipation to see my mom coming out of her bedroom dressed for work. I couldn't wait to see what she was wearing, and she always looked so cute and charming. I remember the different outfits she wore as she worked for the state as a secretary and had to look dressed up and professional, and she always looked beautiful to me. Mom would then sit down with Nanny and me with her cup of coffee and have her cigarette. I would pretend to be just like her, and she would roll up a piece of paper, and I would hold it and pretend it was my cigarette while my nanny and mom would talk about the wishes and what plans would be done when we got home from school and what our chores would be, playing outside, and homework, etc.

I remembered hearing and watching for both my mom and dad returning home from work in the family car, and my dad in his truck which would change through the years. The purple and white convertible and the black and white van where my dad would deliver his meat in and his green pickup truck and the family rambler. I loved playing outside, riding our bikes, and remembering a special memory when Santa brought our bikes at Christmas time. Mine was green, sister Libby's was blue, and brother George got a bright yellow tractor.

My favorite thing to do was to ride my bike. I would spend a lot of time riding my bike with my friends especially on Saturday mornings after cartoons and chores. I would be gone an hour and then I had to return home and check in with everyone before going back outside to continue on with my adventure. Roller skating was the second favorite to do. I still have my skate key that I have saved through the many years. The skate key was used to lengthen and tighten the skate to the shoe called Oxford's back in the day, a term old people would use a lot, and now you know I am an old person, *ha ha ha ha ha.* The metal skate had a screw and nut bolt underneath the skate where it would be used by the flat part of the skate key to extend or lengthen the skate to fit your shoe. The end part of the key was used on the sides of the toe grippers that tightened the grips onto the shoe sole. So the style of the shoe had to have a large ridge around the borders to really grip hold on and the Oxford had very large soles. Quite precise I might add to get on, a triumph actually, and you felt like you really did something great just to get it on.

Off you would go skating on cement walkways, sidewalks, and if you were lucky, you lived by friends who had a connected driveway with their neighbors which made for a large, smooth, no cracks, wide open space of slick smooth cement place to roller skate, or near a school where you had lots of cement or tar to skate on the playground. The worse part of it was when your skate would loosen after a time of skating, and at times, it would literally fall off your shoe, at which time you could walk or limp or drag the skate back to where you could sit down to adjust your skate which was usually a curb of the sidewalk or you could stand out in front of your house and scream, *"Mom!"* so she could come out bend over and put the skate on for you right where you stood.

I had a great mom that would do just that, and as I got older when helping my sister with hers, I realized how hard that must have been on my mom's back to do that for me as it took a while being bent over like that to refit and position the skate while you tried to balance on one foot, and she would have to try and keep you from falling during the process. *Geeeeez*!

Also the skate key had another use when it is not being used for skating. You would keep it on a string worn around your neck so you would not lose it, and it would be handy when needed especially on trips away farther from yelling "*Mom*" when not close to your home or like when at the schoolyard, but it was also a symbol when you had a boyfriend, or he liked you; he would ask you to wear his skate key, and he would wear yours. A sign that he liked you a lot like going steady.

It still amazes me just looking at the skate key; all those memories came back to me when my life was passing through my mind as it was such a special love and time in my life. Then playing Jax came to mind. I played Jax mornings at school recess, afternoons, and on weekends with friends, or for hours just by myself. Flashes of playing on the front porch at Nanny and Pappy's house with my next-door neighbor childhood friend when visiting in the summer. I can still feel the hot porch when we would try and sit down with our shorts on in the hot summer months and we would have to look for a cooler spot like on the cement under the shade trees on the sidewalk.

I then saw myself swinging on my nanny's white picket fence which she was always yelling at us kids "not to do that" along with not standing on the banisters or playing in the mud underneath the water cooler! Then I would see myself along with brother or sister riding our one of a special kind homemade stick horses designed by Pappy. They were detailed by special request of color, a pinto or a palomino? Leather straps and painted eyes complete with ears, and Maine put on painted brown sticks or black to match the horses color that were saved from Nanny's brooms and mops. They were so awesome and handmade carved from Pappy's saw in his workshop. I kept reliving these times of playing Hopscotch, Red-Light Green Light, Mother May I, and Hide-and-Seek; oh, let's not forget Tag,

You're It! Coloring, learning to knit, paper dolls, our walks downtown to the public pool, wearing our flip flops, and grabbing our towels off we would go. Trips to the five-and-tens store with our quarters, our allowance for helping Nana with the laundry and hanging the clothes on the line with clothespins, I remember the smell of the sheets; I remember how fresh they smelled; it would come back to me like I was there again, washing dishes, setting the table, and learning to iron which I still love to do. Rolling on the grass and then itching afterward. Breaking pomegranates on the cement sidewalk so we could eat each seed and then having to hose off the mess with soapy water or just sitting outside on the lawn waving at cars and people passing by or laying on the grass at night and looking up at the stars, oh so many stars and listen to the frogs and the crickets; I remember how good it felt after running thru sprinklers being so wet and then the wonderful feeling of showering and putting on clean dry clothes. Remembering so much of living simple little everyday things would come to me in my dreams.

I really had a super childhood and the pleasures of knowing my cousins, aunties, and uncles, and being able to stay with them and the last-minute plans to go home with them and stay for a week in the summertime! Remembering singing all the way in the car ride three hours to Modesto from Sacramento with my Auntie Bonnie, Uncle Bob, Cousin Kathi, Cousin Chuck, me, my sister, Libby, and brother George; all of us packed into the car with suitcases in the trunk along with theirs and then our parents would pick us up the next week later!

So fun growing up with cousins Cathy, Linda, and Donna at Auntie Evelyn's big house that was just around the corner and up the hill from Nanny and Pappy's house to stay with them for the day or for overnight. The mud pies Cathy and I would make and the playground down at the end of the alley. We loved going down there to play, and we felt so grown-up by going down there by ourselves without any adult supervision. Drinking from the water faucets and playing on the teeter-totter and slides. I remember one time when we were to get our chores done: dusting, clean bathrooms, vacuum, and we could not go to the show or out dancing, unless chores were done by the time my Auntie Evelyn would get home, and I remember waiting to the last minutes completing them as she would open and come thru the front door! I remember her smiling as she knew what we were doing all along. I had the best summers there, and once back home, it would be time to go school shopping.

I went to school in Sacramento; it would start in September! I loved to go school shopping, and we would catch the city bus just down the street from where we lived, and it would drop us off right in front of our house. I remember my favorite store was the Lerner department store where they carried my favorite half sizes like 9–10 and 11–12. The first of its kind for short waisted girls like me! Going to Kmart for lunch, sitting at the circle lunch counter! Having banana splits, toasted turkey and bacon triple stacked sandwiches called the turkey club held together with toothpicks and with colored foils on the tips! Milkshakes and/or Coca-colas, the cherry or vanilla? I remember coming home with all my packages and showing Daddy all our new clothes, and we would give him a fashion show—well, at least my sister and I would as brother George never felt the need to; I mean how exciting is jeans and striped shirts anyway! *Hahaha.*

Never forgetting the smell of the new clothes even now; today, one of my favorite things to do is go shopping. From seeing how everything is displayed especially at Christmas time and how the stores' windows and inside displays were all so different! I remember buying just the right thing for someone special, and then wrapping it in a very special wrapping that would be different each year and couldn't wait for them to open it and see how much they liked it! The candlelight services and dressing up at Easter to go to Church; it was so important and so much fun to look forward to. From my childhood on to remembering all the holidays of doing those things for my own children too as they grew up and remembering all their toys and special shopping sprees, and I'm talking about a lot of holidays; all of this I'm experiencing in my dreams. Then I would dream about my happiest moments of having my children, and the day they were born, the men in my life, to the man I dated and married. My high school chum and the people in my life from kindergarten and on through beauty school to becoming a nanny, and the joy of being grandparents; all of it. My high school years, and both my wedding days, my extended family, and even the houses I have lived in and the people and friends I have made through the years. The salons I worked in: John and Julie's Salon, Ideal Hair, the salon I owned, Creative Hair in Fresno, and Sisters Act with my partner and my sister Libby. Bella Donna and Step-in Out, and The Green Room, and euphoria, Ulta Beauty, and the last salon, Pura Vita. My church and my church family I attended while living in Red Bluff, The First Christian Church, and my long time church family The Congregational Church of Soquel. My Christian teachings and the pastors who taught me the Bible, Dan Woolery and Pastor Mark Fountain. Singing in the choir both times with my high school sweetheart, Dave, and again with Dave as my wonderful Christian husband and the hymns my nana so loved and remember looking up at her as a little girl watching her pray and sing while visiting her Presbyterian Church. The last snowstorm before I got sick, even remembering my favorite books *Johnny Apple Seed*, *The Hardy Boys*, *Little Women*, *Walt Disney's Cinderella*, *Bambi*, *Lady and the Tramp*, and *Peter Pan*. TV shows, Lawrence Welk, and the first time I saw Elvis come on his show! *General Hospital*, *Queens for a Day*, *The Waltons*, *Little House on the Prairie*, *Bonanza*, *Mash*, *The Johnny Carson Here's Johnny!*, and *Saturday Night Live*! All this in a period that I have been told of three weeks when I was on the ventilator!

Was I Being Punished?

The emotions and the questions that filled my mind. Remembering the lessons learned from the stupid mistakes I have made, the things experienced, and the news of disappointments. Having to leave my coastal towns Capitola and Santa Cruz and having to say goodbye to my daughter and grandchildren after years of being there for them. Being their nana was no longer an option due to sudden life changes. Could I stay in my beautiful ocean town? Now experiencing literally possible homelessness and financial despair. Facing the heartbreaking reality that we must move away. Just going through the heartbreak of having to put our golden down, our beloved Eddy, who is fourteen years old; we could no longer watch him suffer from his hip dysplasia, and after hundreds of dollars of meds only to learn that he had liver disease, and that the meds were not working, and the trauma of saying goodbye and then our rents going up. These series of events that forced us to no other choice—we had to leave. Then remembering the day that I got the call from my son; answers came in from hidden past thanks to the DNA found from 23andMe and Ancestry. I learned the truth of add-ons and takeaways in our family history. I remember the shock of hearing the truth of not really knowing for sure; a mystery no longer and secrets that came out news that caused a lot of people great sadness and pain that I never meant to cause. A painful reminder of a young girl's inexperience of being in love; I couldn't help wonder if for all these reasons, I was having to go through this horrible sickness to have time to have to think about all this and feeling like I was being punished. Thank goodness that the love of God was with me, and I realized, that there are no mistakes in life especially when it comes to loving. Things happen for a reason, and I was meant to marry hubby number 1 and to have his children; he probably would never have or the family he was blessed to have! Hubby number 2 and I were destined to be together, soul mates, from love experienced from high school and thirty-three years later now and forever! It was all supposed to happen that way, and I believe life experiences puts you where you are meant to be to meet the people you are meant to meet and to share and be the people you are meant to become. It's all by a great design and all the blessings that come with it!

Thank God that I had my faith, it has sustained me through, and God's grace was with me. All the love I was blessed with, the prayers, money, cards. I am loved by so many. It is no accident that I am here and still here for only the good Lord knows that time and the day, but I will never forget my love from family, and friends, and how being so sick and almost not being here changed my life for the better. As hard as I had to work to get back to the living, it is so worth it. My life and my family's life will never be the same, and we will all look at life a little different now, realizing what is really important. It's not the amount of money you make or where you live or where you come from that defines you. You learn that *life* is the most precious gift on earth.

The day before I left the hospital, I learned the first COVID-19 patient had come into the Asante Hospital. I had wanted to go to the ICU and thank all my nurses and the doctors to give them all hugs and show them what I really looked like when my body that holds my soul is well. At the request of my daughter, she begged me not to as she was so worried that now returning home, I was too vulnerable to be around the COVID-19 patient. Little did I know that the whole world would be staying at home to quarantine and stay safe, hundreds of people just like me were not able to work or leave our homes. We all had to learn what was most important by saving lives that was the most important over money and we truly learned to count our blessings and try to find the good in this crazy time of Corona crisis.

What It Took to Get Home!

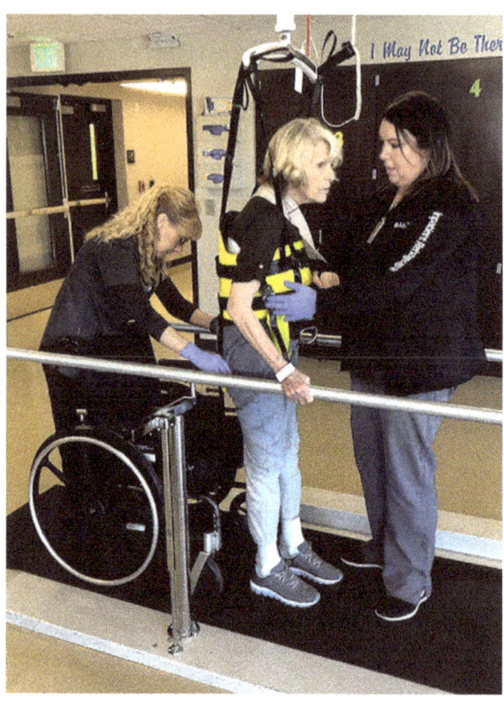

Reflecting back on my journey from ICU to IMCU, from feeling like I was cast in cement and could not move, to be able to move my toes and ankles up and down, the Chelator boots I had to wear to keep my feet straight and out of the covers. I couldn't stand my feet being tucked in under the blankets as I felt trapped.

I remember when they started moving my legs up and down and finally feeling like I could start to move. The first time I sat up took three physical therapists to help me sit on the edge of the bed and help me to stand! I could lift myself up to sit up in bed using just my right hand as my left side is paralyzed. Finding the strength to roll over to use the bed pan. Holding a spoon steady for the first time, learning to eat and drink again, and learning to even sleep in a sling one for day and one for night. Both were very uncomfortable as the wrist brace in the sling would hit my stomach feeding tube, and during any movement, especially in therapy, it would hurt my stomach muscles. The arm sling shoulder strap would go around my neck and then wrap around to my back and help hold me up while being hooked up to lift me up to walk the parallel bars and lift machine even with only my right hand and arm strength. I was remembering the thrill of learning to walk again.

That I could stand even with the help of a lift bar hooked to me felt so good; it made me so happy. Then learning to stand and walk with no lift and trying to stand up straight and not crooked over. I still, to this day, a year later, working on that. I had to learn to sit and wheel myself in the wheelchair and not keep going around in circles as I again only had use of one arm to steer and my legs which I had to learn to use heals to walk and move the chair in balance with each other. I had to learn to transfer on a slide board to transfer from my bed to the wheelchair. Learn to stand by myself and remembering the first time my daughter tried to help me by herself, and I couldn't do it as I had no strength to do it! Learning to stand from bed to walker and over to the bedside potty commode with help lots of help. Being fitted with my new fiberglass leg supports with chelating ankle joints that fit inside my new walking shoes. I learned to stand and walk again on a side bar in a hallway which was a fabulous accomplishment to work my way back home. Walking with my walker counting how many steps.

I remember walking down the long hallway with my wonderful therapists: Gayle, Valery, and Sherri. I will never forget how Valery wheeled me down to the garage at the hospital during my therapy lesson to see my husband Dave, and the car salesman, Matt, to see if I could fit in the car from wheelchair to transfer to inside the car. She sat in the garage in my wheelchair while we did the transfer and said, "Go try out your new car as we hadn't had a chance to test drive it!" Dave made sure getting us this new Chevy Equinox as our Hondas were too low to the ground and too compact of a sport car for me to get in or out of. So off we went with the dealer and had a great test run. It was perfect and so comfortable! Our life travel would be so different now with just one car and so different from our sporty Hondas! My final therapy learning to step in and out of the shower and learn to dress myself! I was going to be ready to go home come hell or high waters; I was going home March 12, 2020, and that is exactly what I did saying goodbye with hugs to my therapists; Dave and the nurses packed me up and wheeled me out to our new car, and I was so happy to have survived, and fifty-eight days later so blessed to be going home!

From day one since I have been home, I have felt the urgency to write my story and especially now with COVID vaccines available to all; it is so important that people get theirs to not only stop this epidemic but to take this information to do whatever it takes to not ever be so sick or cause anyone to be put on a ventilator as a last chance of life support alone and with no one there but the nurses to hold your hand! I also hope that this will help those who had a loved one die or was blessed enough to survive. Know that if you are placed on a ventilator and are in self-induced coma, you can hear people talking then know what they are saying to you because your brain stays alert and stores the information and releases it back to you when you are able to receive it, and you will feel the prayers and the love that is felt there! I want people to know that God is real and that he is there with you always!

March 12, 2020 Going home after 58 days.

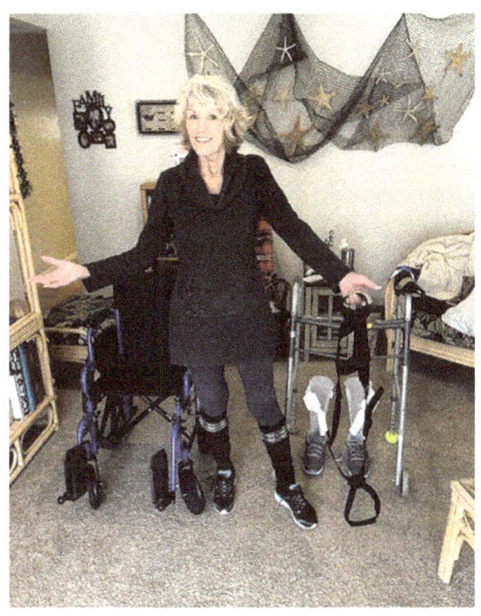

Four months later after rehabilitation, letting go
of all the medical equipment used.

About the Author

B onnie Dunlap is a Christian; she married her high school steady boyfriend thirty-three years after graduating from Ck McClatchy High School. She is a mother of two—a son and a daughter. She is a nanny and a grandma of five and is a great grandma! She is a cosmetologist by trade and has a love for all people. She is a proud member PEO (philanthropist education organization) EQ chapter in Medford, Oregon.

www.ingramcontent.com/pod-product-compliance
Lightning Source LLC
Chambersburg PA
CBHW040117150726
48005CB00013B/1751